A SWIFTLY TILTING SHORE

Seraphim George

ISBN: 979-8-9998878-2-5

♥

To my wife, Juliana.
We walk this tilting shore together.

INTRODUCTION

We are always standing on a shore. Sometimes the ground is steady beneath us; other times it tilts, and the waves threaten to pull us under. Love is the tide that moves us; toward friends, toward lovers, toward God, and it leaves behind both driftwood and treasure on the sand.

The poems in this book follow that tide. It's a collection about love, love of many kinds: the fragile devotion between friends, the consuming and bewildering intensity of romance, and the longing that reaches toward God. For me, these are not separate realms but different shades of the same longing. To love another person, to yearn for the sacred, even to grieve a broken friendship, all are movements of the same heart. It's not tidy, and neither is this book, though I've tried to give it some semblance of order: poems gather into three broad currents of brokenness, passion, and transcendence. Together, they form the shore I have walked and, in some sense, am still walking. And I do not mean these poems as answers, but as markers along the shoreline: fragments of longing, grief, intimacy, and faith. They are the record of a life that has known both absence and presence, silence and song.

The first part of this collection, *Broken Shores*, begins with loss, disillusionment, and the weight of futility. Myth presses against the personal here: Sisyphus pushes his stone, lovers vanish into silence, grief takes its seat at the table. To love is to risk loss, and I wanted these poems to dwell in that space honestly. There is no easy comfort, no premature turning away from the ache of absence. The shore tilts downward here, into the undertow, and the poems sink into it. But even in loss there is a strange kind of clarity, a stripping away that leaves us bare before ourselves.

The second part, *Currents of Desire*, is a turn toward passion. If the first section acknowledges what love can take away, this one dares to say what it gives. Here are poems of intimacy, of erotic longing, of desire both sacred and profane. Love here is flesh, but flesh shot through with fire: at once dangerous and luminous, consuming and generative. I wanted this section to wrestle with the tension between body and spirit, to show how they are not always opposed but sometimes bound up in each other. Desire can lead us astray, but it can also be the place where we are most awake to the divine spark. The poems here ask what it means to call that spark holy.

Finally, the third section, *Pilgrimage of Waves*, turns outward and upward. After loss and desire, what remains? I believe it is love in its more enduring forms: the loyalty of a friend who sits with you in silence, the complicated inheritance of fathers and sons, the longing for God that threads through even our most human loves. This is not an arrival at certainty so much as a widening, an opening into relationship and transcendence. The shore tilts upward here, toward a horizon where human love and divine love touch.

These three movements: loss, passion, transcendence, are not stages to be passed through once and left behind. They circle back, over and over. A friend dies and grief returns. A lover's body awakens the ache again. A prayer, whispered in the night, reminds us that God has been listening all along. To love is to walk a shoreline where the ground is always changing. The tide rushes in, the tide recedes, and we stumble forward again.

A Swiftly Tilting Shore is my attempt to hold those contradictions together, to say that love is never one thing, but many. And perhaps that is the only thing that makes us human: that we keep walking the shore no matter how unsteady, listening for the surf, waiting for what will come in with the tid

TABLE OF CONTENTS

SECTION I
BROKEN SHORES

SISYPHUS

Tribulations endure

Until the gods see us remade

Or see that our remaking is in vain.

What then, when all is lost,

Eternally regretful

At hard-heartedness? Mindless pain

Remains my path, up this crag-mired terrain,

Where when the boulder falls

I pay for all my vices,

Brought from kingship to eternity

In Tartarus, a sweated penalty

Of labor. So be sure

Offenses always come,

But cursed are those by whom they come.

And those who scorn at their mortality,

those who store up vanities,

Prepare yourself for penance.

All your life a joy has hovered

Just beyond the grasp of consciousness.

The day will surely come

When you awake to find

Beyond all hope that it's attained

Or, like me, that it was yours to gain,

And you've lost it, perfectly.

A SWIFTLY TILTING SHORE

He stares across the room
at empty walls. He listens,
waits. He cannot hear her breathe.
He doesn't move,

just stares ahead and listens,
listens, listens, knowing how
she's gone to the black sea
on waves of release,

her color evanesced
to canvas, washed out
and something else changed,
she remained, hollowed.

Now he falls into the sea
from a swiftly tilting shore,
borrowing her fate
to sink, to drown, to feel

into the depth-shrouds
of forgetfulness,
too tired to swim
or build a raft and oar.

SCHADENFREUDE

Thank God he's dead.
I interject
to say again, he's dead;
thank God for that.
Samaritan illusion

came and went, pilfered
by a libertine
anathema: the man
who tripped upon
a rock once thrown

by his own hands,
drowning in his
own bath drawn,
inspired dose
of liquid vengeance.

I would have drawn it
for him, if he hadn't.

SANDY MEDITATION

As I was praying on my sanded shrine,
A hipped girl walked by; a tall, fine specimen,
Who made me wonder if I'll always be
Indebted with the ample price I have to pay
For ruttish sins until I turn to dust,
Or if I'll turn from monkery, to love again.

SHAKESPEARE ON DATING

Suicide, thy name is Woman.

Men have bled into eternity for love,

and am I to be made of stone,

touched by none?

But I have put the knife to work again.

A woman's love bleeds all.

THE CUCKING STOOL

Affliction is the cucking stool of life.
We ensconce ourselves within its torrent,
respire its polluted water, to drown:
a sure end.

I live deformed, unable to sustain
the weight of tribulation, am trampled
by the aching ever-presence, the sin
of ennui,

deceived, saronged by the world's venal yoke.
But my voice remains unburdened, immune
from the resistance of acedia,
so I cry,

wail to the sea and to its god, who hears,
breaking from the depths of my ordeal,
erupting from its adamantine face,
to echo.

LOSS

Sitting on my deck
I look around,
hear the sound
of birds,
intermingled
with the ocean-like
surf song
of stately Oak
and Maple,
shuffling
their branches.

I close my eyes
and realize
that all around
is no relief
from unsustained
and hollow grief.

The neighbor's blinds
are down. Within,
my mother sings.
The trees are blind,
the birds dumb,

the wind deaf
as it carries off
my prayers, draws them
from my breath
to unseen,
unknown ears.

At least alone
this truth is sure:
sun, shade, wind,
bird and butterfly
can't stab you
in the back or lie.

They don't save face.

LOVED AND LOST

I

Whoever said,
Tis better to have loved and lost,
than never to have loved at all'?

Liar. You have never loved.

Or loved and never lost,
rested in her cantrip arms,
lighthouse to the lost lover's ship.
They beckoned you like rays of light,
puncturing your soul like knives
through the emptiness of night.
But you rested on their edges,
steel-cold to the vagabond's touch,
soothing to love's fire cracking
in the embers of your heart,
and then you wrote those lies.

But I have lost.

I don't believe your poetry,
your fanciful imagination.

I have lost.

II

Love is, for me, a threadless needle,
a coat with none to wear it
though the world is frigid,
a sea, its waves tumultuous,
symphonic, swirling up, around
like a conductor's wand
yet heard by none,
received by nothing:
there is no sand, no splash, no ears.

A tree falls in a forest,
a man falls for a woman,
but if there are none to hear it
has he ever loved at all?

Yes. Oh yes, and how he loved.

But better if he hadn't.

NEW YEAR'S EVE

Night dawns another new year
and eve the end of one,
the light undone
with failure in its wake.

Moon-beams haunt my window pane,
breathe the frost, casting halos
through New England air.
In another year, will I sit

to write another poem
of another New Year's Eve,
having phoenixed
through the ashes of a lost cause?

SECTION II
CURRENTS OF DESIRE

AN ACT OF MARRIAGE

Sear it forever in my mind,
and let it radiate from there,
a sun to warm
my ice soul-nights.

Persevering to remember
this guignol act, played out for me,
two wood-beams merged,
forever joined

in the Golgotha of my mind,
the fell, on which you died instead:
two beams, never
to be divorced.

Let me hear throughout the ages
that ceremony's wedding bells.
Let them free me
with their ringing.

A RIPARIAN DRAMA

Hermaphroditus and the nymph
exchange their glances,
passing by like lovers
impassioned by the fervid sun.

She drags her blue and milky hand
across his talus skin,
stroking, turning his face
though still but not unmoved, entranced

by the pounding of her steps,
the ripples of her dress
that fruitlessly obscure
her body's taut, quivering contours.

He draws her in until they kiss
upon a bed of sand
and pulse and roll and move
upon and in each other, one.

AN ADMIRATION

If you turn your face,

I'll admire your feet,

feet smudged by pavement and rain,

ankles sore from subway stairs,

your body balanced

on blistered arches.

Sacred wanderer,

I know your face.

Your eyes, lit like storefront glass,

spill their honey

into the night air,

sweet against the grit.

But I admire your feet.

I love your feet

because they carried you

through laundromats and bus stations,

over bridges rinsed in headlights,

through broken glass and summer weeds,

until they found me.

DIVINE VOYEUR

But that is what I hear, told she's coming,
and God is in it too. I hope it's true,
that lust lived out in white will then be mine.
But on that hallowed night let's not bring up
the fact that He'll be there.

We are galvanized, actuated heat,
impassioned sweat and fragrant moist release
of guimpe and alb, indulgent fever pitch
and soul egalitarianism.
It's odd to contemplate

He's in this moment, though we shouldn't mind.
I mind. To think, I call Him father,
not a sex-crazed and nymph-like deity
more fitting found in paganistic rite.
My father hoists me up

in muscled arms. I wait with bated breath,
as through a sea of stars and dappled blue
He moves me, away from perverse frictions,
toward a different kind of life, a night
where she, who is faceless,

lies nude and shadowed by his pearl-light moon.

My desire suits this. He sets me down

beside His flesh-robed soul reflection,

a generous perfection, poised, like me

in bed, and makes us whole.

DON'T TELL ME THAT I'M YOUNG

I'm young.

As if I cannot feel the airborne sting
of a million locust thoughts.
They pester me, a young choice grain
that stands in solitude.

I'm young.

As if the weight of tired years at twenty six
is feather-lite, not weighty as the night.

I'm young.

As if a man, bloated and distorted,
drowned in his own tears
at twenty six feet deep
is less drowned than one at forty.

That's why I wait for you, my love,
at twenty six years young.
If you are God, then come.
If Eve, then I will wait until I wake.

21

Are you young, too?

Then come and pick these grains
with gleaning hands
before the coming of the years.

Don't tell me that I'm young.

DREAMING HARLEQUIN

Awake I am
the dreaming harlequin,
and nightmares face
my wan reflection,
wandering
their evanescent
shadows.

Asleep I live
in glad forgetfulness
and wake to keep
in quiet solitude,
escaping
the image of a man
to be one.

DRIVING

Headlights battle the indifferent night,
while here, I'm lost in thought, in deed, in sight.

Outside my window, shadows fly behind
and catch my stare. I turn my head and mind
to he who drives, and all looks fine.

All did, back when the strain upon the air
first throttled me with thick philosophy,
amplified the melancholy drone
of my friend, driving.

What? Could this, our night, be ruined by unwelcome
thoughts?
          Yes, and trampled, spit upon, and bent
to be removed, along with joy and gratitude,
replaced, outdone in bluest griefly hue
of wounds lanced and pouring out forgotten woes.

My God, the guy could act like all was well.
But I know better still.

Silence cannot bully me aside. This way
I'll play along and gaze at widening road,

24

at flying shadow and indifferent night,

bidding quietude to dry the tear,

caught with my eye's corner, on his hand and wiped away.

Two men together on a lonely road,

one heart breaking, another understanding,

the broken man driving.

We've stopped.

You're home and it's goodbye, I guess.

I'd stay and talk, even though there's nothing

I can do. My door slams, and his does too.

I could give a hug, not like a woman's,

conceded, but love still needed.

Headlights battle the indifferent night,

while here, I'm lost in thought.

My turn to drive.

A DRYAD IN WINTER

It seems like only yesterday I saw
a dryad dancing in the bloom of Spring,
and captured it, became its lover
when I took you by the arm and led you
out among the amaranthine flowers.

I was happy to have lived for years
within you, years that ever-came in waves
crashing over Summer waves: warm, constant,
making me forget the season's turning
and your waning's inexorable approach.

You remained the defining fragrance
of an autumn leaf that, with earthen smell
and color-blast undoes the growing dread
of Winter, comforting beneath my shoes,
echoing the hush of the first Fall-frost.

And I was happy, drifting off to sleep,
perchance to dream of your crystalline face,
still beside me, glass upon the surface,
a quiet lake enveloped by the moonlight
of another wadmal Winter's night.

DEVICES AND DESIRES

Forgive, Almighty and most Merciful,
for I have sinned and strayed like wayward sheep.

With her I was mistaken, mistaken,
and this perfect trinity of disillusion
moved upon the surface of the deep.
Mistaken, though I met her in a church,
and watched her silently, unwilling to disturb
the prayers that, for me, were sacred.
The chalice of her lips; the halos
floating in her eyes, brown like the mud
placed by Christ upon the beggars lids
to sanctify his sight, though she was blind;
her face, reminiscent of the Panaghia.
Because of these and many other things,
I could have sworn . . .

But she was Ishtar, mother of the gods,
prima donna, venerated saint, then diva
teaching me her liturgy,
her capacity for solace,
reliquary to my loneliness,
and in the end she gave me nothing
but abandonment and heartache,

yet I saw her in a church,

that pall face covering a world of pretense

and I could have sworn . . .

But I found a sad reality instead,

driven by my heart's devices and desires

to rely upon this delicate deception.

Only God knows why He placed her where I tread,

a path that led to death or reformation.

Lord, have mercy, sinner that I am,

confessing all his faults and penitent.

With her I was mistaken.

A LOVE POEM

They say that we are not the same,
that your life and mine will be lost,
that I am nothing, and you are everything,
that two such different persons cannot love.
But I will not forget I loved you once,
that you will love me still,
and I still long to die within your arms.

I cannot comprehend their judgments,
their cold philosophies, rendered meaningless,
undone by first love's light.

Together we should confiscate the present
from our enemies, escape to dwell
where none can judge,
where none can say it isn't true,
where milk cascades from skeletal goats
and honey from the rock.

We must flee, exiled from the world,
to where there is no law,
only love.

MY FATHER'S SON

I'm my father's son,

and he, his son's father.

Could the logic be any simpler,

the equation any more manifest?

Yet I cannot grasp it

with my mind. Cannot

plumb the depths

of its significance.

SECTION III

PILGRIMAGE OF WAVES

EVERMORE BY DAY

The night, a cloak of finest threads of shade
Against this beacon fights, which I believe
Is weak. The moon of self-will, which does achieve
A month, is inconstant as light's masquerade.

O moon, I've lost your light which once did aid
This traveler who, upon a winter's eve
Fell into the shadow, which you did weave
Along the way, and despaired when light did fade.

So I will travel ever more by day,
Who's light is strong, not mixed with darkened night,
And shining longer makes the road a quicker way,
So I can rest when fades the greater light,
And turning from the moon of self I may
Receive the sun of truth and with it sight.

ICEBERG

I reek of breaking,

float alone in Arctic fathoms,

a danger to all

who see the tip,

my visible being

the self

who sails upon its antipode.

Circumnavigate

my borders, but stave your way

or risk the gauntlet

of my presence:

shepherding the loss

of souls

to a Protean persona.

But the sun melts

at times. It warms above the waves,

and then I roll,

the weight of me,

the stark threat of edge

exposed

until I've gone to water,

able to lift men up,

not drag them down.

INTO THE WARDROBE

I

You were standing there.
The party over,
silence filled your house,
in a peopled place
now filled with empty plates
and hollow glasses,
humming conversations'
echo ringing in your ears.
You were standing there.
At the threshold,
after stumbling
down the steps I turned
and saw you smiling,
reminding me
you've made a lasting
love and memory,
and you'll be on your way.
I wondered when
this wanderlust
came knocking at your door,
settled in your hearts
to beckon you

into the wardrobe,
out onto an open
everlasting road.

II

It stands before you now. Heavy wooden doors,
dark with mystery, carved in fine designs
of choices made and chiseled memory,
summon you to open them and journey through.
You can smell the air. It shouldn't be there,
foreign to a closet where for years
you've hung your heavy coats. It smells of change.
It smells of coast and waves, of pallid moonlight,
early morning rain, aromatic meadows
crowned with rocks thrust miles to the heavens,
with all the other wonders you will find.

You take a step, push through your lifeless
old and moldy clothes, and there it is:
a light that blinds, soaks you in a brighter sun,
'till you adjust to see the land spread out
to misted valleys, where the air is fresh,
spellbound, and discovery is breath.
You'll be spirited away until pursuit
succumbs to destiny in that faire state,

cared for by a great majestic king,

where the wind blows at his mane's shake,

and, at his roar, the earth quakes.

He's on the move.

III

As a thousand years is like a day,

those months will seem to you when you have reigned

upon that castled hill of liberty.

Look down on all you've done to see the way,

a journey home grown thick and overgrown

to stumble back through tear-stained wooden doors,

and all the fast-forgotten memories

won, regained to coalesce once more,

but only after struggling through coats

and scents you've left behind, you'll turn and seal

the doors. But though you will have traveled

there and back again, remember where you've been,

for like that never-ending sky, the road
you travel here at home will never end.

LEAVING ARMAGEDDON

When I'm older, I will say
that I was handsome once,
when you didn't love me.

I saw you in a hundred faces,
pursued you, through dry and arid places,
where moth and rust and vultures
picked my bones
till I was withered dry.

So rise with Spirit-breath
in Armageddon, rise
with sinew, flesh and life
by the calling of the man of God,
and we will leave this place

together.

THE ONLY THING BETWEEN US

I

The run down joint barely stood out
on Main Street, among shops
and fancier places to eat
with less food for more money.

But we went, and what we lacked
in glitz, we gained in time well spent.
He played it straight, hard-assed, macho
as always, from his speech, his drinks,

all of his remembered days
of school-yard fights and lots of girls,
military drills and war,
every muscled push through life

another score on the board
of manhood. He wished I had more points.
He wished more often I had tossed
the coins of risk. He has some left.

II

I had to laugh a little
at all his complications,
imagining inside
are implications

flying high within his mind,
of me, a faithful kowtow boy,
never falling from the nest,
obdurate as stone,

and there he is, alone
on see-saws, swings, and Ferris wheels,
the dance floor, the bathroom floor,
intelligent enough

to deal with all the issues
spinning round his head,
glimpsed like blurring faces
from a merry-go-round.

Despite the news, luminous,
pressing to denude itself,
I will remain a child,
sparing him the anguish

of broken ice, and hearing
all about the wonder years
I've had to live without,
so I just sit and smile.

III

I noticed your graying hair,
your silent film gestured
quasi- paternal face,
know-it-all eyes,

your hard nose, sharp lips spewing
patriarchy wisdom,
a fortune cookie
once resented.

This time, as we retreat
into the Cape Cod night
and down the crowded street,
I walk beside you.

I'm right where you are,
confident the only thing
that stands between us now
is your goodbye.

THE PRAYER

She is inviolate and poised
upon the precipice.
The rock rises up, catches her
and she, though still, journeys,
set like the masthead of a ship,
withstanding the maelstrom.

Her hair entangles with the wind
like a thousand flags of peace
beneath the nettled firmament.
Dressed in black, enveloped
in the yare wings of a blackbird
flapping, pulling, pushing

up, up, up, and higher still
ever nearer Heaven.
Her hands are clasped below her waist
simply, at rest, closed
like her eyes. She is seeing God,
hearing His call: fly! Fly!

The elements swirl around her,
drawing up her prayers,
a murmur grown into a Voice

to the One who hears.

And her words, pledged, petitioned,

chase the wind, availing much.

THE WAY IT IS

My lids are heavy still, but useful,

peering through my lack of sleep at sandy-hair

and sandy eyes; we're both well-worn.

The light, a growing saffron glow,

reflects your earnest face, a mouth that chews your thoughts

and spits them out in prayer and ennui:

as it should be.

Friends as brothers, reminiscing;

times like this come few and far between.

The clock and breath and life go on,

as do our many words released into the troposphere,

soaked up, received by God.

Tennis-matched ideas

                 are tossed between us.

Good intentions, volleyed aspirations

fly contained within each played-out ball,

and in this match our hearts and skills become refined,

born of different blood yet blood-born kin the same in time.

Wait.

Can it be? The match complete already?

Borrowed time is burning steady still,
and yet, I better go,

although, I wish you'd stay,
a rook among the pawns
upon the chessboard
of the White King watching,
for another game, another day.

But what will be your strategy?
Where, now, will you move?

Getting up, the lawn chair creaks beneath me;
trees rustle, birds sing, but silence closes in.
Near the gate I turn to you and say unsure,
See you next week and nothing more.
Words cannot express what friendship understands.

I close the gate and sigh, tired but at peace.

APOCALYPSE

My body trembles, wracked with earthquake-sobs,

breaking bone and crust and sinew,

beating waves through every earthen member:

child lost, a love abandoned,

truth - the glorious Son of God revealed,

and the world groans.

Foundations reel,

earth's blood seethes,

fire and water,

ash and smoke,

a darkened sun,

a reddened moon,

tormented souls,

weeping, gnashing,

the ground contorts

and folds.

I call to the mountains and rocks

to fall on me; they don't.

I search for death and endless peace

to bury me; it won't.

Its anger pounds me still

and crushes innards into dust

until, I'm left un-filled.
The waters of the deep burst forth.
The tremor strikes again.
The tremor strikes again,
and again,
and again,
and again.

But then,

clouds part, illumination breaking through,
and He appears, that secret lover, who
adorns the bride with joy, like birth pang's past,
descending on the ruins of the old at last.

ABOUT THE AUTHOR

Seraphim George's work bridges nature, faith, and the human experience. He has published poetry in multiple literary journals and wrote an award-winning novel. Seraphim continues to write poetry and novels while working in Communications for non-profit organizations. He spends his free time in church, on the water, and in the written word, not to mention raising his three children with his wife, Juliana, and his cat, Kimchi. *A Swiftly Tilting Shore* is his second poetry collection.

To read more of his work and find out more, visit www.seraphimgeorge.com.